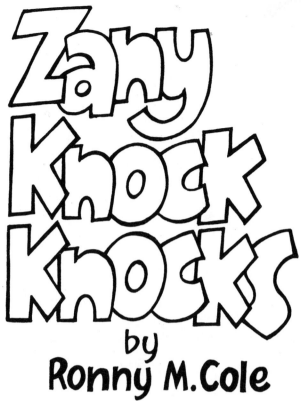

Zany Knock Knocks

by
Ronny M. Cole

ILLUSTrated by
Rich Garramone

 Sterling Publishing Co., Inc. New York

To Adam and Arielle

Library of Congress Cataloging-in-Publication Data

Cole, Ronny M.
    Zany knock-knocks / Ronny M. Cole ; illustrated by Rick Garramone.
        p.   cm.
    Includes index.
    Summary: A collection of knock-knock jokes arranged alphabetically.
    ISBN 0-8069-8588-7
    1. Knock-knock jokes.   2. Wit and humor, Juvenile.   [1. Knock-knock
jokes.   2. Jokes.]   I. Garramone, Rick, ill.   II. Title.
PN6231.K55C65   1993
818'.5402—dc20   92-43068
                                                                                            CIP
                                                                                             AC

Cover design by Sanford Hoffman

10   9   8   7   6   5   4   3   2   1

Published in 1993 by Sterling Publishing Company, Inc.
387 Park Avenue South, New York, N.Y. 10016
Text © 1993 by Ronny M. Cole
Illustrations © 1993 by Rick Garramone
Distributed in Canada by Sterling Publishing
% Canadian Manda Group, P.O. Box 920, Station U
Toronto, Ontario, Canada M8Z 5P9
Distributed in Great Britain and Europe by Cassell PLC
Villiers House, 41/47 Strand, London WC2N 5JE, England
Distributed in Australia by Capricorn Link Ltd.
P.O. Box 665, Lane Cove, NSW 2066
Manufactured in the United States of America
All rights reserved

Sterling ISBN 0-8069-8589-5 Paper
            ISBN 0-8069-8588-7 Trade

A

Knock-knock.
  Who's there?
Aaron.
  Aaron who?
Why Aaron you
opening the door?

Knock-knock.
  Who's there?
Abe.
  Abe who?
Abe out face!

Knock-knock.
  Who's there?
Abe Lincoln.
  Abe Lincoln who?
Abe Lincoln
(a blinkin') yellow
light means slow down!

Knock-knock.
  Who's there?
Abercrombie.
  Abercrombie who?
Abercrombie (have a crumby)
time at the party!

Knock-knock.
  Who's there?
Abyssinia.
  Abyssinia who?
Abyssinia at the mall!

Knock-knock.
  Who's there?
Acey Ducey.
  Acey Ducey who?
Acey your point,
Ducey mine?

Knock-knock.
  Who's there?
Adam.
  Adam who?
Adam my way—
I'm coming in!

Knock-knock.
  Who's there?
A La Mode.
  A La Mode who?
Remember the A La Mode (Alamo)!

Knock-knock.
  Who's there?
Aldous.
  Aldous who?
Aldous fuss over
little ol' me?

Knock-knock.
  Who's there?
Aldus.
  Aldus who?
Aldus talk
and no action!

Knock-knock.
  Who's there?
Alice.
  Alice who?
Alice fair in love and war!

Knock-knock.
 Who's there?
Alistair.
 Alistair who?
You uncover the pot, Alistair the soup!

 Knock-knock.
  Who's there?
 Altoona.
  Altoona who?
 Altoona piano—you play it!

  Knock-knock.
   Who's there?
  Brinckerhoff.
   Brinckerhoff who?
  You Brinckerhoff the soda—
  I'll bring the other half.

Knock-knock.
 Who's there?
Alma.
 Alma who?
The dog ate Alma
homework!

Knock-knock.
  Who's there?
Amana.
  Amana who?
Amana-eating tiger!

Knock-knock.
  Who's there?
Camellia.
  Camellia who?
Camellia little
closer.

  Knock-knock.
    Who's there?
  Meteor.
    Meteor who?
  Prepare to Meteor (meet your) maker!

Knock-knock.
  Who's there?
Amahl.
  Amahl who?
Amahl tied up,
call me later!

Knock-knock.
　Who's there?
Amarillo.
　Amarillo who?
Amarillo nice guy.

Knock-knock.
　Who's there?
Amerigo.
　Amerigo who?
Amerigo-round.

　Knock-knock.
　　Who's there?
Vespucci.
　Vespucci who?
How much is Vespucci (that poochie)
in the window?

Knock-knock.
　Who's there?
Arcudi.
　Arcudi who?
Arcudi little dog
can do one trick.

Knock-knock.
  Who's there?
Annapolis.
  Annapolis who?
Annapolis day keeps the doctor away.

Knock-knock.   Knock-knock.
  Who's there?   Who's there?
Angela.   Anita.
  Angela who?   Anita who?
Angela Mercy.   Anita rest!

Knock-knock.
  Who's there?
Anna Mary.
  Anna Mary who?
"Anna Mary old
soul was he . . ."

Knock-knock.
  Who's there?
Antilles.
  Antilles who?
Antilles open the door,
I'm gonna sit here on your doorstep!

8

Knock-knock.
  Who's there?
Ariel.
  Ariel who?
You're Ariel pain in the neck!

  Knock-knock.
    Who's there?
  Cosmo.
    Cosmo who?
  You Cosmo trouble
  than you're worth!

Knock-knock.
  Who's there?
Amish.
  Amish who?
Amish you sho mush!!

Knock-knock.
  Who's there?
Armstrong.
  Armstrong who?
Armstrong as an ox—
and you have the brain
of one.

  Knock-knock.
    Who's there?
  Arsenio Hall.
    Arsenio Hall who?
  Arsenio Hall (I've seen you all) over town!

9

Knock-knock.
 Who's there?
Artichoke.
 Artichoke who?
Artichoke on a
chicken bone.

Knock-knock.
 Who's there?
Artie Fish.
 Artie Fish who?
Artie Fish-el
intelligence!

Knock-knock.
 Who's there?
Aruba.
 Aruba who?
Aruba (are you the) one in charge?

Knock-knock.
 Who's there?
Ashley.
 Ashley who?
Ashley, I'm not sure . . .

Knock-knock.
 Who's there?
Asbestos.
 Asbestos who?
I'm doing Asbestos I can!

Knock-knock.
  Who's there?
Astoria.
  Astoria who?
I've got Astoria wouldn't believe!

  Knock-knock.
    Who's there?
  Boris.
    Boris who?
  Go ahead, Boris with another story!

Knock-knock.
  Who's there?
Attila.
  Attila who?
Attila we meet again!

Knock-knock.
  Who's there?
Aubrey.
  Aubrey who?
Aubrey Quiet!

Knock-knock.
  Who's there?
Auerbach.
  Auerbach who?
Please scratch
Auerbach.

Knock-knock.
   Who's there?
Auletta.
   Auletta who?
Auletta bygones be bygones!

Knock-knock.
   Who's there?
Auntie.
   Auntie who?
Auntie Aircraft!

Knock-knock.
   Who's there?
Avalon.
   Avalon who?
Avalon way to go!

Knock-knock.
   Who's there?
Avenue.
   Avenue who?
Avenue any pity?

Knock-knock.
   Who's there?
Ayatollah.
   Ayatollah who?
Ayatollah you to keep
your hands to yourself!

B

Knock-knock.
 Who's there?
Babbit.
 Babbit who?
Babbit and Costello!

Knock-knock.
 Who's there?
Bach.
 Bach who?
Bach to the future!

Knock-knock.
 Who's there?
Baldoni.
 Baldoni who?
Baldoni a
little on
the top.

Knock-knock.
 Who's there?
Barbara.
 Barbara who?
The Barbara Seville.

Knock-knock.
  Who's there?
Bea.
  Bea who?
Bea Faroni!

Knock-knock.
  Who's there?
Bee Hive.
  Bee Hive who?
Bee Hive yourself!

Knock-knock.
  Who's there?
Betty.
  Betty who?
Betty B. Careful!

Knock-knock.
  Who's there?
Blake.
  Blake who?
Blake a leg!

Knock-knock.
  Who's there?
Brigham.
  Brigham who?
Brigham a present!

Knock-knock.
  Who's there?
Bruno.
  Bruno who?
Bruno who it is!

Knock-knock.
  Who's there?
Buck and Ham.
  Buck and Ham who?
Buck and Ham Palace!

Knock-knock.
  Who's there?
Butcher.
  Butcher who?
"Butcher head on my shoulder . . ."

C

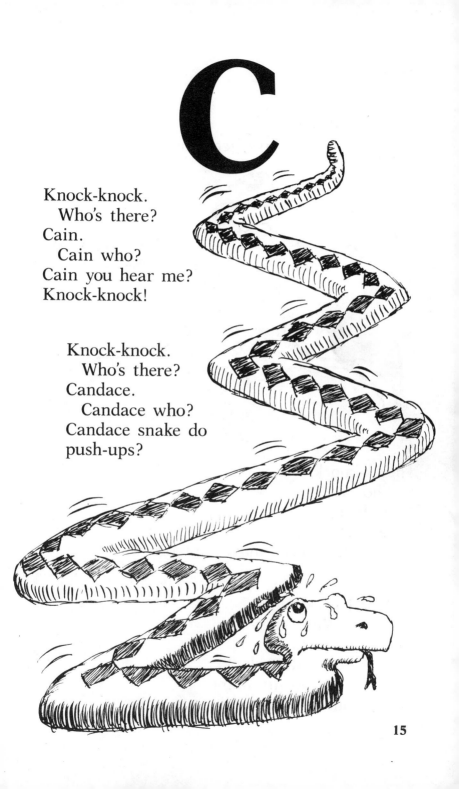

Knock-knock.
  Who's there?
Cain.
  Cain who?
Cain you hear me?
Knock-knock!

  Knock-knock.
    Who's there?
  Candace.
    Candace who?
  Candace snake do
  push-ups?

15

Knock-knock.
  Who's there?
Cannibal.
  Cannibal who?
Cannibal (can a bull) ice skate?

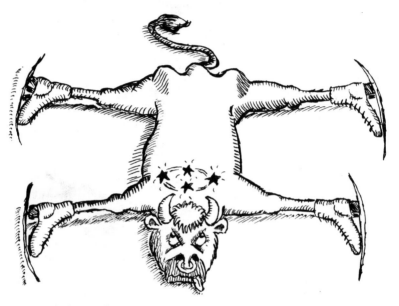

Knock-knock.
  Who's there?
Cantaloupe.
  Cantaloupe who?
Cantaloupe today, maybe tomorrow . . .

        Knock-knock.
          Who's there?
        Cantillo.
          Cantillo who?
        Cantillo my name,
        but my face will be familiar.

Knock-knock.
 Who's there?
Carmen.
 Carmen who?
" 'Carmen to my parlor,'
said the spider to the fly!"

Knock-knock.
 Who's there?
Carrie.
 Carrie who?
Carrie R. pigeon.

Knock-knock.
 Who's there?
Casanova.
 Casanova who?
Casanova (isn't over)
until the fat lady sings.

Knock-knock.
 Who's there?
Cashew.
 Cashew who?
Cashew see I'm busy?

Knock-knock.
 Who's there?
Cass.
 Cass who?
Cass Toff, we're leaving!

Knock-knock.
  Who's there?
Cassie.
  Cassie who?
Cassie Nova! How can you resist me?

  Knock-knock.
    Who's there?
  Will F.
    Will F. who?
  Will F. Iron.

Knock-knock.
  Who's there?
Cassie.
  Cassie who?
Cassie O. Watch!

Knock-knock.
  Who's there?
Cassie.
  Cassie who?
Cassie you now—
I've got to run!

Knock-knock.
  Who's there?
Cassius.
  Cassius who?
Cassius if you can!

  Knock-knock.
    Who's there?
  Cattle Drive.
    Cattle Drive who?
  This Cattle (cat will) Drive you crazy!

Knock-knock.
 Who's there?
Celeste.
 Celeste who?
Celeste you know the better!

Knock-knock.
 Who's there?
Cher.
 Cher who?
Cher would be nice if you opened the door!

Knock-knock.
 Who's there?
Cherry.
 Cherry who?
Cherry Lewis!

Knock-knock.
 Who's there?
Chester.
 Chester who?
Chester little kid!

Knock-knock.
 Who's there?
Chicken.
 Chicken who?
Just Chicken
out the
doorbell!

Knock-knock.
  Who's there?
Coed.
  Coed who?
Coed (go ahead),
make my day!!

Knock-knock.
  Who's there?
Cohen.
  Cohen who?
Cohen home—goodbye!

  Knock-knock.
    Who's there?
  Cummings.
    Cummings who?
  Cummings back tomorrow!

Knock-knock.
  Who's there?
Coincidental.
  Coincidental who?
Coincidental (go in the dental) chair
and have your teeth cleaned.

Knock-knock.
  Who's there?
Count Aaron.
  Count Aaron who?
Count Aaron-telligence.

Knock-knock.
  Who's there?
Crassus.
  Crassus who?
Crassus always greener on the other side!

Knock-knock.
  Who's there?
Culligan.
  Culligan who?
I'll Culligan when you have
something intelligent to say.

  Knock-knock.
    Who's there?
Culver.
    Culver who?
Culver me up, I'm freezing.

Knock-knock.
  Who's there?
Czar.
  Czar who?
Czar-y about that!

  Knock-knock.
    Who's there?
  Apollo.
    Apollo who?
  Apollo G. Accepted!

D

Knock-knock.
  Who's there?
Dakar.
  Dakar who?
Dakar has a flat tire!

Knock-knock.
  Who's there?
Dakota.
  Dakota who?
Dakota many colors.

Knock-knock.
  Who's there?
Damascus.
  Damascus who?
Damascus slipping
off da face.

Knock-knock.
  Who's there?
Dancer.
  Dancer who?
"Dancer, my friend, is blowing in the wind . . ."

Knock-knock.
  Who's there?
Daniella.
  Daniella who?
Daniella (don't yell at) me, I can hear you!

22

Knock-knock.
  Who's there?
Darren.
  Darren who?
Darren you to open the door!

    Knock-knock.
      Who's there?
    New Year.
      New Year who?
    New Year (knew you were)
    going to say that!

Knock-knock.
  Who's there?
Deanne.
  Deanne who?
I'm Deanne-sir to your prayers!

    Knock-knock.
      Who's there?
    Gallo.
      Gallo who?
    Gallo your dreams

Knock-knock.
  Who's there?
Morgan.
  Morgan who?
Morgan just a pretty face!

Knock-knock.
  Who's there?
Dee Wallace.
  Dee Wallace who?
"Dee Wallace came tumbling down!"

  Knock-knock.
    Who's there?
  Eye Sore.
    Eye Sore who?
  Eye Sore them coming!

Knock-knock.
  Who's there?
Diane Kilburn.
  Diane Kilburn who?
"Diane Kilburn's (the ankle bone's)
connected to the foot bone..."

  Knock-knock.
    Who's there?
  Dog Catcher.
    Dog Catcher who?
  Dog Catcher (don't count your)
  chickens before they hatch!

24

Knock-knock.
  Who's there?
Donald.
  Donald who?
Donald (don't hold) your breath!

Knock-knock.
  Who's there?
Don Blaine.
  Don Blaine who?
Don Blaine (don't blame) me!

Knock-knock.
  Who's there?
Don Boris Witty.
  Don Boris Witty who?
Don Boris Witty details!

Knock-knock.
  Who's there?
Don Marcus.
  Don Marcus who?
Don Marcus absent, we're right here!

Knock-knock.
  Who's there?
Donovan.
  Donovan who?
Donovan think about it!

Knock-knock.
  Who's there?
Dona Lewis.
  Dona Lewis who?
Dona Lewis (don't lose) your temper!

Knock-knock.
  Who's there?
Donna.
  Donna who?
"Way Donna-pon the Swanee River . . ."

Knock-knock.
  Who's there?
Doris.
  Doris who?
Doris no fool like an old fool!

Knock-knock.
  Who's there?
Dozer.
  Dozer who?
Dozer the breaks!

Knock-knock.
  Who's there?
Dragon.
  Dragon who?
Quit Dragon your
tail!

  Knock-knock.
    Who's there?
Autumn.
    Autumn who?
You Autumn mind
your own business!

Knock-knock.
  Who's there?
Dudes.
  Dudes who?
Dudes and don'ts.

Knock-knock.
  Who's there?
Duncan.
  Duncan who?
Duncan Donuts.

27

Knock-knock.
  Who's there?
Druscilla.
  Druscilla who?
Druscilla (drew a silly)
picture of the teacher.

  Knock-knock.
    Who's there?
  Mamie.
    Mamie who?
  She Mamie erase it.

Knock-knock.
  Who's there?
Dwayne.
  Dwayne who?
"Dwayne in Spain falls
mainly in the plain ..."

  Knock-knock.
    Who's there?
  Wayne.
    Wayne who?
  "Wayne, Wayne, go away,
  come again another day!"

E

Knock-knock.
  Who's there?
Eiffel Tower.
  Eiffel Tower who?
Eiffel (I feel) Towerble!

  Knock-knock.
    Who's there?
  Elaine.
    Elaine who?
  Elaine down
  to take a nap.

    Knock-knock.
      Who's there?
    Ma Belle.
      Ma Belle who?
    Ma Belle E. aches.

      Knock-knock.
        Who's there?
      Cara Mia.
        Cara Mia who?
      Cara Mia to the doctor!

Knock-knock.
  Who's there?
Emma Lou King.
  Emma Lou King who?
Emma Lou King into my crystal ball . . .

Knock-knock.
  Who's there?
Emma.
  Emma who?
Emma Nemms!

Knock-knock.
  Who's there?
Encino.
  Encino who?
Hear no evil, speak
no evil, Encino evil!

Knock-knock.
  Who's there?
Enid Sue.
  Enid Sue who?
Enid Sue like a
hole in the head!

Knock-knock.
  Who's there?
Errol.
  Errol who?
Errol be a hot time in the old town tonight!

Knock-knock.
  Who's there?
Estelle.
  Estelle who?
Estelle am waiting for you to open this door!

Knock-knock.
  Who's there?
Etta May Whit.
  Etta May Whit who?
Etta May Whit- (At my wits') send!

Knock-knock.   Knock-knock.
  Who's there?   Who's there?
Etta.   Eubie.
  Etta who?   Eubie who?
Etta Boy!   "Eubie long to me . . ."

Knock-knock.
  Who's there?
Eudora Belle.
  Eudora Belle who?
Eudora Belle thing, you!

    Knock-knock.
      Who's there?
    Goddess.
      Goddess who?
    Goddess stop meeting like this.

Knock-knock.
  Who's there?
Eudora.
  Eudora who?
Eudora is stuck!

Knock-knock.
  Who's there?
Europe.
  Europe who?
Europe (you're up)
to no good!

Knock-knock.
  Who's there?
Evan.
  Evan who?
Evan Lee coffee!

Knock-knock.
  Who's there?
Ewell.
  Ewell who?
Ewell catch more flies
with honey than with vinegar!

F

Knock-knock.
 Who's there?
Fallacy.
 Fallacy who?
I Fallacy (fail to see)
what's so funny!

Knock-knock.
 Who's there?
Fanny.
 Fanny who?
Fanny you should ask!

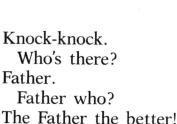

Knock-knock.
 Who's there?
Far Side.
 Far Side who?
As Far Side (far as I) know, it's still me!

Knock-knock.
 Who's there?
Farrah.
 Farrah who?
Farrah 'n wide.

Knock-knock.
 Who's there?
Father.
 Father who?
The Father the better!

Knock-knock.
  Who's there?
Fatso Kay.
  Fatso Kay who?
Fatso Kay with you, Fatso Kay with me!

Knock-knock.
  Who's there?
Ferrara.
  Ferrara who?
"Long ago and Ferrara-way . . ."

Knock-knock.
  Who's there?
Fiendish.
  Fiendish who?
Fiendish your dinner!

Knock-knock.
  Who's there?
Fission.
  Fission who?
Fission for compliments!

Knock-knock.
  Who's there?
Fitzhugh.
  Fitzhugh who?
If the shoe Fitzhugh wear it!

Knock-knock.
  Who's there?
Flaherty.
  Flaherty who?
Flaherty will get you nowhere!

Knock-knock.
  Who's there?
Florist.
  Florist who?
You can't see the
Florist for the trees!

Knock-knock.   Knock-knock.
  Who's there?   Who's there?
Fonzi.   Ford.
  Fonzi who?   Ford who?
Fonzi meeting you here!   Ford-y thieves.

Knock-knock.
  Who's there?
Foreign.
  Foreign who?
"Foreign twenty blackbirds baked in a pie ..."

Knock-knock.
  Who's there?
Formosa.
  Formosa who?
Formosa my life, I've been waiting for you to open the door!

Knock-knock.
  Who's there?
Fred.
  Fred who?
Fred I'll have to tell you another joke. . . .

Knock-knock.
  Who's there?
Freeze.
  Freeze who?
"Freeze a jolly good fellow . . ."

Knock-knock.
  Who's there?
Frieda.
  Frieda who?
Who's a Frieda the big bad wolf?

    Knock-knock.
      Who's there?
    Doughnut.
      Doughnut who?
    Doughnut be afraid—it's only me!

G

Knock-knock.
  Who's there?
G-Man.
  G-Man who?
G-Man-y Crickets!

Knock-knock.
  Who's there?
Galahad.
  Galahad who?
I knew a Galahad
two left feet!

Knock-knock.
  Who's there?
Garcia.
  Garcia who?
Garcia (go see) the principal.

Knock-knock.
  Who's there?
Garter.
  Garter who?
Garter go now!

Knock-knock.
  Who's there?
Gauguin.
  Gauguin who?
Gauguin, it's your turn!

Knock-knock.
  Who's there?
Gavin.
  Gavin who?
Gavin you one more chance
to open the door!

    Knock-knock.
      Who's there?
    Dustin.
      Dustin who?
    Dustin off the battering ram!

        Knock-knock.
          Who's there?
        Germaine.
          Germaine who?
        Germaine (you're mean)
        to act this way!

Knock-knock.
  Who's there?
Gibbon.
  Gibbon who?
Are you Gibbon me trouble?

    Knock-knock.
      Who's there?
    Gil Diaz.
      Gil Diaz who?
    Gil Diaz (guilty as) charged!

Knock-knock.
  Who's there?
GM.
  GM who?
GM I rattling your cage?

Knock-knock.
  Who's there?
Goddard.
  Goddard who?
You Goddard be kidding!

Knock-knock.
  Who's there?
Aikido.
  Aikido who?
Aikido you not!

Knock-knock.
  Who's there?
Goody.
  Goody who?
"Goody-vening!" says Count Dracula.

    Knock-knock.
      Who's there?
    Venom.
      Venom who?
    Venom I going to get inside?

      Knock-knock.
        Who's there?
      Vicious.
        Vicious who?
      Best Vicious!

Knock-knock.
  Who's there?
Gray Z.
  Gray Z. who?
Gray Z. mixed-up kid!

Knock-knock.
  Who's there?
Guava.
  Guava who?
Guava good time!

Knock-knock.
  Who's there?
Guinesss.
  Guinness who?
Guinness a break!

Knock-knock.
  Who's there?
Giuseppe.
  Giuseppe who?
Giuseppe (just stepped) in
something on your doorstep.

  Knock-knock.
    Who's there?
  Houdini.
    Houdini who?
  Houdini that thing on your doorstep?

Knock-knock.
  Who's there?
Gummy.
  Gummy who?
Gummy five!

Knock-knock.
  Who's there?
Gwynn N.
  Gwynn N. who?
Gwynn N. bear it!

41

H

Knock-knock.
 Who's there?
Habit.
 Habit who?
Habit your own way!

        Knock-knock.
         Who's there?
        Hair Combs.
         Hair Combs who?
        Hair Combs the Judge!

Knock-knock.
  Who's there?
Harrison.
  Harrison who?
Harrison idea—you tell the next joke!

Knock-knock.
  Who's there?
Hartley.
  Hartley who?
This is Hartley the time
to be telling knock-knock jokes!

Knock-knock.
  Who's there?
Ed Rather.
  Ed Rather who?
Ed Rather be sailing!

Knock-knock.
  Who's there?
Harv and Hugh.
  Harv and Hugh who?
Harv and Hugh (haven't you) got a minute?

Knock-knock.
  Who's there?
Hedda.
  Hedda who?
Hedda I win, tails you lose!

Knock-knock.
  Who's there?
Healy.
  Healy who?
Healy my pain . . .

Knock-knock.
  Who's there?
Heidi.
  Heidi who?
Heidi go seek.

Knock-knock.
  Who's there?
Hello Etta.
  Hello Etta who?
"Hello Etta, gentille Alouetta . . ."

Knock-knock.
  Who's there?
Hiram.
  Hiram who?
Hiram glad you asked!

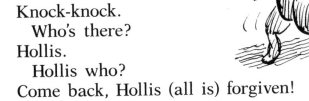

Knock-knock.
  Who's there?
Hollis.
  Hollis who?
Come back, Hollis (all is) forgiven!

Knock-knock.
  Who's there?
Honda.
  Honda who?
Honda road again!

Knock-knock.
  Who's there?
Honorless.
  Honorless who?
Honorless you open this door,
I'll have to break it down!

Knock-knock.
  Who's there?
Hoodoo.
  Hoodoo who?
Hoodoo you want it to be?

  Knock-knock.
    Who's there?
  San Juan.
    San Juan who?
  San Juan (someone) else!

  Knock-knock.
    Who's there?
  Asta.
    Asta who?
  Asta La Veesta, baby!

Knock-knock.
  Who's there?
Horace.
  Horace who?
Horace of a different color!

Knock-knock.
  Who's there?
House.
  House who?
House it going?

Knock-knock.
  Who's there?
Howard.
  Howard who?
Howard you like to crawl
back under your rock?

Knock-knock.
  Who's there?
Hubie Maddern.
  Hubie Maddern who?
Hubie Maddern
a wet hen!

Knock-knock.
  Who's there?
Hugo N.
  Hugo N. who?
Hugo N. Crazy—
and I'm goin' home.

Knock-knock.
  Who's there?
Hyam Alda.
  Hyam Alda who?
Hyam Alda washed up!

I

Knock-knock.
  Who's there?
Ice Water.
  Ice Water who?
My Ice Water
when I chop onions!

Knock-knock.
  Who's there?
Icon.
  Icon who?
Icon live without you!

Knock-knock.
  Who's there?
Ida Clair.
  Ida Clair who?
Ida Clair, you're the
most stubborn person!

Knock-knock.
  Who's there?
Ida Klein.
  Ida Klein who?
Ida Klein to answer
that question!

Knock-knock.
  Who's there?
Iodine.
  Iodine who?
Iodine (I'm a dyin') for a pizza!

Knock-knock.
  Who's there?
Iris.
  Iris who?
Iris I could rock you to sleep—
with big ones!

Knock-knock.
  Who's there?
Cotton.
  Cotton who?
Cotton off to a bad start!

Knock-knock.
  Who's there?
Combat.
  Combat who?
Combat tomorrow!

Knock-knock.
  Who's there?
Isabelle.
  Isabelle who?
Isabelle broken?

Knock-knock.
  Who's there?
Isadore.
  Isadore who?
Isadore stuck?

Knock-knock.
  Who's there?
Isaiah.
  Isaiah who?
Isaiah there, old chap,
why don't you open the door?

Knock-knock.
  Who's there?
Istanbul.
  Istanbul who?
Istanbul fight over?

Knock-knock.
  Who's there?
Ivan.
  Ivan who?
"Ivan working on the railroad . . ."

J

Knock-knock.
  Who's there?
Jack N.
  Jack N. who?
Jack N. the Box.

Knock-knock.
  Who's there?
Jackel.
  Jackel who?
Jackel lantern.

Knock-knock.
  Who's there?
Janet R.
  Janet R. who?
Janet R. in a drum.

Knock-knock.
  Who's there?
Jeff.
  Jeff who?
Jeff Boy-R-Dee.

Knock-knock.
  Who's there?
Jericho.
  Jericho who?
Jericho to Disneyland?

Knock-knock.
  Who's there?
Jerome.
  Jerome who?
Have it Jerome way!

Knock-knock.
 Who's there?
Jess B.
 Jess B. who?
Jess B. Cuzz!

Knock-knock.
 Who's there?
Jess Horace.
 Jess Horace who?
Jess Horace-n' around!

Knock-knock.
 Who's there?
Jester.
 Jester who?
Jester minute, I've got more
knock-knock jokes!

Knock-knock.
 Who's there?
Jethro.
 Jethro who?
Jethro (just throw)
me a few bones.

Knock-knock.
 Who's there?
Jock.
 Jock who?
Jock-late milk shake.

Knock-knock.
 Who's there?
Juan.
 Juan who?
Juan good turn deserves another!

Knock-knock.
  Who's there?
Juan.
  Juan who?
Juan two, buckle my shoe . . .

    Knock-knock.
      Who's there?
    Grigor.
      Grigor who?
    Grigor (three, four), shut the door . . .

Knock-knock.
  Who's there?
Physics.
  Physics who?
Physics (five, six), pick up sticks.

    Knock-knock.
      Who's there?
    Stefan Haight.
      Stefan Haight who?
    Stefan Haight, lay them straight.

Knock-knock.
  Who's there?
Jubilee.
  Jubilee who?
Jubilee-ve in the tooth fairy?

K

Knock-knock.
  Who's there?
Kareem Cohen.
  Kareem Cohen who?
Ice Kareem Cohen!

Knock-knock.
  Who's there?
Karen.
  Karen who?
Karen-teed to crack you up!

Knock-knock.
  Who's there?
Keith.
  Keith who?
Keith me, you fool!

Knock-knock.
  Who's there?
Ken D.
  Ken D. who?
Ken D. gram.

Knock-knock.
  Who's there?
Kiefer.
  Kiefer who?
Kiefer stiff upper lip.

53

Knock-knock.
  Who's there?
Kenya.
  Kenya who?
Kenya hear me knocking?
I said "Knock-knock!"

Knock-knock.
  Who's there?
Kevin.
  Kevin who?
"Thank Kevin
for little girls . . ."

Knock-knock.
  Who's there?
Klaus.
  Klaus who?
Klaus your mouth and open the door!

Knock-knock.
  Who's there?
Koala.
  Koala who?
Koala-T jokes like these are hard to find.

Knock-knock.   Knock-knock.
  Who's there?   Who's there?
Kris.   Kurt.
  Kris who?   Kurt who?
Kris P. Critters!   Kurt that out!

54

L

Knock-knock.
  Who's there?
L.B.
  L.B. who?
L.B. the judge of that!

Knock-knock.
  Who's there?
Leah Penn.
  Leah Penn who?
Leah Penn Lizards!

Knock-knock.
  Who's there?
Lettuce.
  Lettuce who?
Lettuce discuss this like mature adults ...

Knock-knock.
  Who's there?
Linda.
  Linda who?
Linda helping hand.

    Knock-knock.
      Who's there?
    Yukon.
      Yukon who?
    Yukon count on me.

Knock-knock.
  Who's there?
Lionel.
  Lionel who?
Lionel get you in trouble!

Knock-knock.   Knock-knock.
  Who's there?   Who's there?
Lucy.   Luke.
  Lucy who?   Luke who?
Lucy Nupp!   Luke out below!

    Knock-knock.
      Who's there?
    Lyndon.
      Lyndon who?
    Lyndon Ear!

M

Knock-knock.
  Who's there?
Mabel.
  Mabel who?
Mabel I'll tell you and Mabel I won't!

Knock-knock.
  Who's there?
Mack.
  Mack who?
Mack up your mind!

Knock-knock.
  Who's there?
Madge.
  Madge who?
Madge N. that!

Knock-knock.
  Who's there?
Ma Harrison.
  Ma Harrison who?
Ma Harrison (my hair is on) fire!

Knock-knock.
  Who's there?
Mannheim.
  Mannheim who?
Mannheim tired!

Knock-knock.
  Who's there?
Manny Dunn.
  Manny Dunn who?
Manny Dunn
grow on trees.

Knock-knock.
  Who's there?
Mansion.
  Mansion who?
Did I Mansion I have
more knock-knock jokes?

Knock-knock.
  Who's there?
Marsha.
  Marsha who?
Marsha Mallow!

Knock-knock.
  Who's there?
Math.
  Math who?
Math (mashed) Potatoes!

Knock-knock.
  Who's there?
May Kay.
  May Kay who?
May Kay while the sun shines!

Knock-knock.
  Who's there?
Mazda.
  Mazda who?
Mazda of the Universe!

Knock-knock.
  Who's there?
Midas.
  Midas who?
Midas well try again—knock-knock!

      Knock-knock.
        Who's there?
      Mike Rowe.
        Mike Rowe who?
      Mike Rowe wave oven.

Knock-knock.
  Who's there?
Missouri.
  Missouri who?
Missouri (misery) loves company!

  Knock-knock.
    Who's there?
  William.
    William who?
  William miss me when I'm gone?

      Knock-knock.
        Who's there?
      Mischief.
        Mischief who?
      I guess I'd Mischief (miss you if)
      you left . . .

N

Knock-knock.
  Who's there?
Nanya.
  Nanya who?
Nanya Lip!

Knock-knock.
  Who's there?
Narragansett.
  Narragansett who?
Narragansett (never
can sit) still in class!

Knock-knock.
  Who's there?
Needle.
  Needle who?
Needle little help!

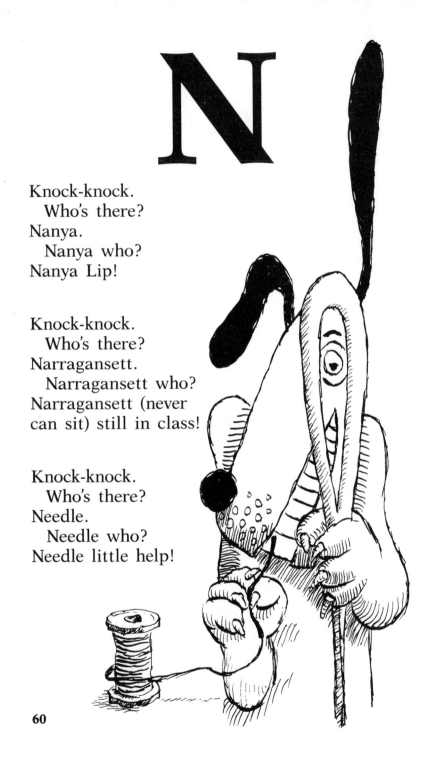

Knock-knock.
  Who's there?
Nefertiti.
  Nefertiti who?
Nefertiti (never teeter) totter
with a 500-pound gorilla!!

Knock-knock.
  Who's there?
Albee.
  Albee who?
Albee a monkey's uncle!

Knock-knock.
  Who's there?
Nemo.
  Nemo who?
Nemo time to think
of a joke!

Knock-knock.
  Who's there?
Noah.
  Noah who?
There's Noah-scape!

Knock-knock.
  Who's there?
Nevada.
  Nevada who?
You Nevada had it so good!

    Knock-knock.
      Who's there?
    Gouda.
      Gouda who?
    This is as Goudas it gets!

        Knock-knock.
          Who's there?
        Osgood.
          Osgood who?
        Osgood S. Canby.

Knock-knock.
  Who's there?
Nora Marx.
  Nora Marx who?
Nora Marx (no remarks)
from the peanut gallery!

    Knock-knock.
      Who's there?
    Avery.
      Avery who?
    Avery body's gettin' into the act!

O

Knock-knock.
  Who's there?
O'Casey.
  O'Casey who?
O'Casey if I care!

Knock-knock.
  Who's there?
O'Keefe.
  O'Keefe who?
"O'Keefe me a
home where the
buffalo roam . . ."

63

Knock-knock.
  Who's there?
Obi Wan.
  Obi Wan who?
Obi Wan-derful and
take me to the movies!

Knock-knock.
  Who's there?
Odaris.
  Odaris who?
Odaris a bee on
your shoulder!

Knock-knock.
  Who's there?
Odd Thing.
  Odd Thing who?
Odd Thing (I'd sing)
all day if I knew a thong!

        Knock-knock.
          Who's there?
        Odyssey.
          Odyssey who?
        Odyssey (hard to see) how you made
        it past the first grade!

Knock-knock.
  Who's there?
Offer.
  Offer who?
Offer Got (I forgot)!

Knock-knock.
  Who's there?
Oink.
  Oink who?
Oink L. Sam!

Knock-knock.
  Who's there?
Olivia.
  Olivia who?
Olivia lone if that's
what you want!

Knock-knock.
  Who's there?
Nevil.
  Nevil who?
Nevil mind!

Knock-knock.
  Who's there?
Otto.
  Otto who?
Your bell is
Otto order.

Knock-knock.
  Who's there?
Owen Williams.
  Owen Williams who?
Owen Williams (oh, when
will you) open this door?

P

Knock-knock.
 Who's there?
Panda.
 Panda who?
Panda monium!

Knock-knock.
 Who's there?
Pasta.
 Pasta who?
Pasta pizza under the door—I'm starved!

Knock-knock.
 Who's there?
Azenauer.
 Azenauer who?
Azenauer (has an hour) gone by
since you put the pizza in the oven?

Knock-knock.
  Who's there?
Pasteur.
  Pasteur who?
It's Pasteur (past your) bedtime!

Knock-knock.
  Who's there?
Patton.
  Patton who?
Patton leather shoes!

Knock-knock.
  Who's there?
Paul.
  Paul who?
Paul-tergeist!

Knock-knock.
  Who's there?
Peapod.
  Peapod who?
I don't want to hear a
Peapod (peep out of) you!

Knock-knock.
  Who's there?
Percy.
  Percy who?
Percy-veere (persevere)!

Knock-knock.
  Who's there?
Phyllis.
  Phyllis who?
Phyllis in on the details!

Knock-knock.
  Who's there?
Pinafore.
  Pinafore who?
Pinafore for your thoughts . . .

Knock-knock.
  Who's there?
Pitcher.
  Pitcher who?
Pitcher money where your mouth is!

Knock-knock.
  Who's there?
Pizza.
  Pizza who?
Pizza nice guy when you get to know him.

Knock-knock.   Knock-knock.
  Who's there?   Who's there?
Police.   Police.
  Police who?   Police who?
Police B. Careful!   Police open the door!

Knock-knock.
  Who's there?
Polly N.
  Polly N. who?
Polly N. saturated.

Knock-knock.
  Who's there?
Porsche.
  Porsche who?
Porsche me in the right direction!

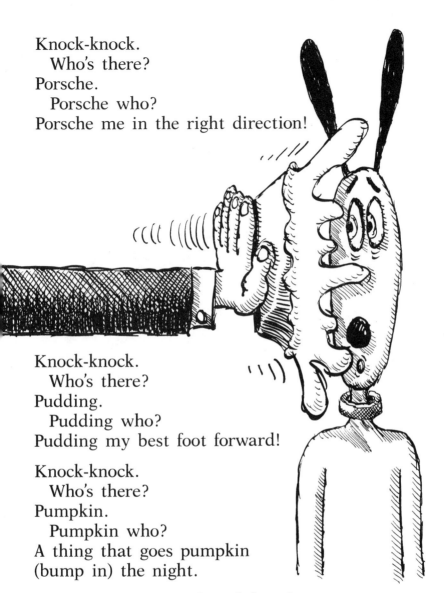

Knock-knock.
  Who's there?
Pudding.
  Pudding who?
Pudding my best foot forward!

Knock-knock.
  Who's there?
Pumpkin.
  Pumpkin who?
A thing that goes pumpkin
(bump in) the night.

Knock-knock.
  Who's there?
Pyrite.
  Pyrite who?
Pyrite in your face—Pow!

69

Q

Knock-knock.
  Who's there?
Quibble.
  Quibble who?
Quibble and Bits.

Knock-knock.
  Who's there?
Quigley.
  Quigley who?
Open the door Quigley, I must get in!

Knock-knock.
  Who's there?
Wilson.
  Wilson who?
Wilson body let me in?

R

Knock-knock.
  Who's there?
Raisin.
  Raisin who?
Raisin Cane!

Knock-knock.
  Who's there?
Rajah.
  Rajah who?
Rajah Rabbit!

Knock-knock.
  Who's there?
Rambo.
  Rambo who?
"Somewhere, over the Rambo . . ."

Knock-knock.
  Who's there?
Ray and Greta.
  Ray and Greta who?
You'll Ray Greta asking me that!

Knock-knock.
  Who's there?
Renata.
  Renata who?
Renata (run out of) steam?

Knock-knock.
  Who's there?
Rhett.
  Rhett who?
Rhett-urn of the Jedi.

Knock-knock.
  Who's there?
Rick.
  Rick who?
Rick Shaw,
hop in for a ride!

Knock-knock.
  Who's there?
Rise and Follow.
  Rise and Follow who?
Rise and Follow (rise and fall of)
the Roman Empire.

Knock-knock.
  Who's there?
Rita.
  Rita who?
Rita my lips!

Knock-knock.
  Who's there?
Robert de Niro.
  Robert de Niro who?
Robert de Niro, but he's not here yet.

Knock-knock.
  Who's there?
Robert Redford.
  Robert Redford who?
Robert Redford the part in the play.

    Knock-knock.
      Who's there?
    Romanoff.
      Romanoff who?
    There ain't Romanoff for the
    both of us in this town!

Knock-knock.   Knock-knock.
  Who's there?   Who's there?
Ron.   Ronan.
  Ron who?   Ronan who?
Ron for your life!   Ronan amuck!

Knock-knock.   Knock-knock.
  Who's there?   Who's there?
Roy.   Russ.
  Roy who?   Russ who?
Roy L. Flush!   Russ Crispies!

Knock-knock.
  Who's there?
Safaris.
  Safaris who?
Safaris I can see, it's me!

Knock-knock.
  Who's there?
Santucci.
  Santucci who?
Santucci my sunburn!

Knock-knock.
  Who's there?
Santa.
  Santa who?
Santa Mental Fool!

Knock-knock.
  Who's there?
Sasha.
  Sasha who?
Sasha dummy!

Knock-knock.
  Who's there?
Saul and Terry.
  Saul and Terry who?
Saul and Terry confinement!

Knock-knock.
  Who's there?
Saul Upp.
  Saul Upp who?
Saul Upp to you!

Knock-knock.
  Who's there?
Schenectady.
  Schenectady who?
Schenectady (the neck of the) shirt is
too tight.

Knock-knock.
  Who's there?
Scoot.
  Scoot who?
Scoot to be here!

Knock-knock.
  Who's there?
Scott.
  Scott who?
Scott to be me!

Knock-knock.
  Who's there?
Sea Bass.
  Sea Bass who?
Sea Bass-tian the crab.

Knock-knock.
  Who's there?
Shafter.
  Shafter who?
Shafter make a phone call!

Knock-knock.
  Who's there?
Shelby and Carmen.
  Shelby and Carmen who?
"Shelby Carmen round the mountain
when she comes!"

Knock-knock.
  Who's there?
Shelley.
  Shelley who?
Shelley try again?

    Knock-knock.
      Who's there?
    Dozen.
        Dozen who?
    Dozen matter to me!

Knock-knock.
  Who's there?
Shopper Dan.
  Shopper Dan who?
You're Shopper Dan
(sharpen than) I thought!

Knock-knock.
  Who's there?
Sloan.
  Sloan who?
Sloan (slow and) steady wins the race!

Knock-knock.
  Who's there?
Sly Dover.
  Sly Dover who?
Sly Dover, I'm breaking down the door!

76

Knock-knock.
  Who's there?
Sodium.
  Sodium who?
Sodium (so do you) mind if I come in?

Knock-knock.
  Who's there?
Sonny N.
  Sonny N. who?
Sonny N. clear today—rain tomorrow!

Knock-knock.
  Who's there?
Wanda.
  Wanda who?
Wanda come out and play?

Knock-knock.
  Who's there?
Sony.
  Sony who?
Sony your old pal . . .

Knock-knock.
  Who's there?
Trotter.
  Trotter who?
Trotter remember me.

Knock-knock.
  Who's there?
Spetzel.
  Spetzel who?
Spetzel delivery!!

Knock-knock.
  Who's there?
Spook.
  Spook who?
I Spook too soon!

Knock-knock.
  Who's there?
Stan and Bea.
  Stan and Bea who?
Stan Dupp and
Bea Counted!

Knock-knock.
  Who's there?
Surreal.
  Surreal who?
Surreal pleasure to be here!

Knock-knock.
  Who's there?
Sven.
  Sven who?
Sven are you going to open the door?

T

Knock-knock.
  Who's there?
Tamara.
  Tamara who?
Tamara Boom-dee-ay!

          Knock-knock.
            Who's there?
          Tennessee.
            Tennessee who?
          Is that a Tennessee (tan I see),
          or haven't you bathed lately?

Knock-knock.
  Who's there?
Tess Slater.
  Tess Slater who?
Tess Slater than
you think!

Knock-knock.
  Who's there?
The Genius.
  The Genius who?
The Genius (the genie is) out of the bottle.

Knock-knock.
  Who's there?
The Ghost.
  The Ghost who?
The Ghost is clear—let's go!

Knock-knock.
  Who's there?
Threadbare.
  Threadbare who?
Threadbare-n (the Red Baron)
and Snoopy the Flying Ace.

Knock-knock.
  Who's there?
Thud.
  Thud who?
Thud you'd never ask!

      Knock-knock.
        Who's there?
      Thurston.
        Thurston who?
      Thurston for some water!

Knock-knock.
  Who's there?
Tijuana.
  Tijuana who?
Tijuana try for two out of three?

80

Knock-knock.
  Who's there?
Tom Hills.
  Tom Hills who?
Tom Hills (time heals) all wounds!

Knock-knock.
  Who's there?
Tommy.
  Tommy who?
I have a Tommy Ache!

Knock-knock.
  Who's there?
Toreador.
  Toreador who?
Toreador down—
now can I come in?

Knock-knock.
  Who's there?
Top Hat.
  Top Hat who?
Top Hat (stop that)—you're bothering me!

Knock-knock.
  Who's there?
Triton.
  Triton who?
"Triton remember the
kind of September . . ."

Knock-knock.
  Who's there?
Troy.
  Troy who?
Troy again!

  Knock-knock.
    Who's there?
  Wes D.
    Wes D. who?
  Wes D. point?

Knock-knock.
  Who's there?
Truman E.
  Truman E. who?
Truman E. cooks spoil the broth!

U

Knock-knock.
  Who's there?
Udder.
    Udder who?
Udder Lee ridiculous!

Knock-knock.
  Who's there?
Uganda.
    Uganda who?
Uganda be kidding me!

Knock-knock.
  Who's there?
Unaware.
  Unaware who?
Your Unaware has
a hole in it!

  Knock-knock.
    Who's there?
Tom Sawyer.
    Tom Sawyer who?
Tom Sawyer
underwear!

Knock-knock.
  Who's there?
Esau.
  Esau who?
Esau it too.

Knock-knock.
  Who's there?
Unique.
  Unique who?
Why do Unique (you sneak)
around on tiptoe?

          Knock-knock.
            Who's there?
          Uta May.
            Uta May who?
          Going Uta May mind!

V

Knock-knock.
  Who's there?
Vacancy.
  Vacancy who?
Vacancy (we can see) right in your window!

Knock-knock.
  Who's there?
Valley.
  Valley who?
Valley intellesting!

Knock-knock.
  Who's there?
Vanna White.
  Vanna White who?
Vanna White (want to write) your name
on this dotted line?

Knock-knock.
  Who's there?
Vasilli.
  Vasilli who?
Vasilli (what a silly) person you are!

Knock-knock.
  Who's there?
Vaudeville.
  Vaudeville who?
Vaudeville (what will) you be doing tonight?

Knock-knock.
  Who's there?
Vaughn.
  Vaughn who?
Vaughn to come over tomorrow?

Knock-knock.
  Who's there?
Vehicle.
  Vehicle who?
Don't call us—
Vehicle (we will call) you!

Knock-knock.
  Who's there?
Ventriloquist.
  Ventriloquist who?
Ventriloquist-mas tree get decorated?

Knock-knock.
  Who's there?
Veronica.
  Veronica who?
Veronica (we're on a c-)razy diet.

86

Knock-knock.
  Who's there?
Vi.
  Vi who?
Vi not?!

Knock-knock.
  Who's there?
Vile.
  Vile who?
Vile the cat's
away, the mice
vill play!

Knock-knock.
  Who's there?
Vilma.
  Vilma who?
Vilma dreams come true?

Knock-knock.
  Who's there?
Waddle.
  Waddle who?
Waddle I need to do to get you
to use your brain?

Knock-knock.
  Who's there?
Waiter.
  Waiter who?
Waiter-ound and you'll see!

Knock-knock.
  Who's there?
Walter D.
  Walter D. who?
Walter D. Lawn.

Knock-knock.
  Who's there?
Wanda.
  Wanda who?
Wanda these days—Pow!

Knock-knock.
  Who's there?
Warden.
  Warden who?
Warden the world are you up to?

Knock-knock.
  Who's there?
Warren.
  Warren who?
I'm Warren out!

Knock-knock.
  Who's there?
Warren D.
  Warren D. who?
Warren D. world are you?

Knock-knock.
  Who's there?
Wash Out.
  Wash Out who?
Wash Out, I'm coming in!

Knock-knock.
  Who's there?
Water.
  Water who?
Water friends for?

Knock-knock.
  Who's there?
Wayne.
  Wayne who?
I'm Wayne D. Outfield.

Knock-knock.
  Who's there?
Wire.
  Wire who?
Wire we telling knock-knock jokes?

    Knock-knock.
      Who's there?
    Wooden.
      Wooden who?
    Wooden you like to know!

      Knock-knock.
        Who's there?
      Wienie.
        Wienie who?
      Wienie more jokes like these!

        Knock-knock.
          Who's there?
        Archibald.
          Archibald who?
        Archibald real tears when he
        read these knock-knock jokes.

    Knock-knock.
      Who's there?
    Woody.
      Woody who?
    Woody lady of the house
    please open the door?

X

Knock-knock.
  Who's there?
X.
  X who?
X (Eggs) Benedict!

Knock-knock.
  Who's there?
Xavier.
  Xavier who?
Xavier self!

Knock-knock.
  Who's there?
Xenia.
  Xenia who?
Xenia open the door last week!

  Knock-knock.
    Who's there?
  Oh Mama!
    Oh Mama who?
  Oh Mama-stake (oh, my mistake)!

Y

Knock-knock.
  Who's there?
Yates.
  Yates who?
Crazy Yates (Eights)!

Knock-knock.
  Who's there?
Yogurt.
  Yogurt who?
Yogurt to be joking!

Knock-knock.
  Who's there?
Arno.
  Arno who?
Arno you don't!

Knock-knock.
  Who's there?
Yokohama.
  Yokohama who?
Yokohama (you can have my) place in line!

Knock-knock.
  Who's there?
Yolette.
  Yolette who?
Would Yolette me in the door, please?

  Knock-knock.
    Who's there?
Wilma.
  Wilma who?
Wilma jokes make you open the door?

    Knock-knock.
      Who's there?
Ozzie.
    Ozzie who?
Ozzie (I see) I'm going to be
out here all night.

      Knock-knock.
        Who's there?
Yukon.
      Yukon who?
Yukon say that again!

Knock-knock.
  Who's there?
Yukon.
  Yukon who?
Yukon (you can't) teach
an old dog new tricks!

Z

Knock-knock.
  Who's there?
Zany.
  Zany who?
Zany body out there?!

Knock-knock.
  Who's there?
Zelda.
  Zelda who?
Zelda family jewels!

Knock-knock.
  Who's there?
Zinc.
  Zinc who?
Zinc or swim!

Knock-knock.
Who's there?
Zits.
Zits who?
Zits down
and concentrate.

Knock-knock.
Who's there?
Zoe.
Zoe who?
Zoe (so we)
meet again!

Knock-knock.
Who's there?
Zoo.
Zoo who?
Zoo long for now!

Knock-knock.
Who's there?
Cy.
Cy who?
Cy O'Nara (Sayonara)!

Knock-knock.
Who's there?
Ollie-Lou.
Ollie-Lou who?
Ollie-Lou ya! You finally
opened the door!

Knock-knock.
Who's there?
Vienna.
Vienna who?
Zis is Vienna the book.

Index of Subjects and Hidden Names

STACKS